Little Fish
and Big Fish

'Little Fish and Big Fish'
An original concept by Lou Treleaven
© Lou Treleaven

Illustrated by Dean Gray

Published by MAVERICK ARTS PUBLISHING LTD

Studio 3A, City Business Centre, 6 Brighton Road,

Horsham, West Sussex, RH13 5BB

© Maverick Arts Publishing Limited July 2017

+44 (0)1403 256941

A CIP catalogue record for this book is available at the British Library.

ISBN 978-1-84886-292-0

Maverick
arts publishing
www.maverickbooks.co.uk

Yellow

This book is rated as: Yellow Band (Guided Reading)
This story is decodable at Letters and Sounds Phase 3.

Little Fish and Big Fish

by **Lou Treleaven**
illustrated by **Dean Gray**

Little Fish and Big Fish

go for a swim.

Little Fish is little.

Big Fish is big.

"I am the biggest fish in the sea," says Big Fish.

A rock moves.

It is not a rock. It is a fish.

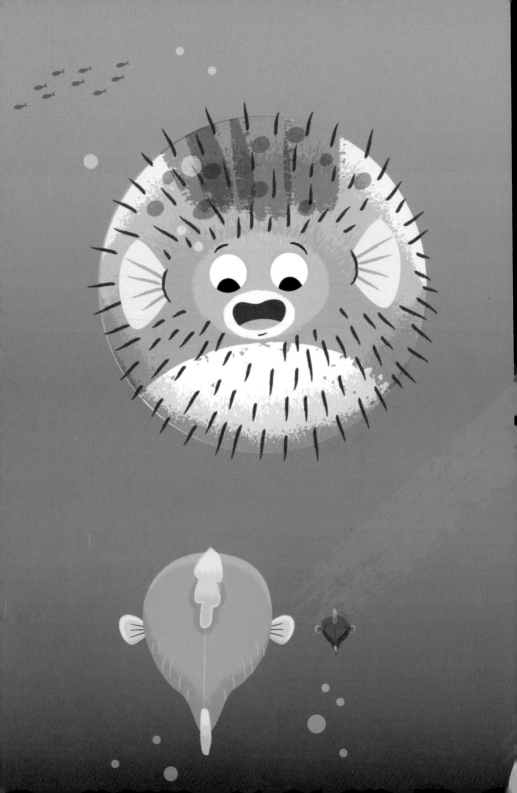

"I am the **biggest** fish in the sea," says the very big fish.

A boat moves.

It is not a boat. It is a fish.

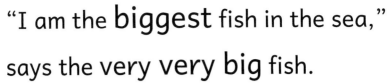

"I am the **biggest** fish in the sea," says the very **very big** fish.

They swim to a cave.

It is not a cave. It is a fish.

"I am the **biggest** fish in the sea,"

says the very **very very big** fish.

"And you will all be my supper!"

"Not me," says Little Fish.

Little Fish gets in a shell.

"Ow!" says a little crab.

"You sat on me, you big, big fish!"

Quiz

1. What do Little Fish and Big Fish do?
a) Have supper
b) Go for a swim
c) Go to sleep

2. It is not a rock. It is...?
a) A crab
b) A shell
c) A fish

3. Where do the fish swim to?
a) A boat
b) A rock
c) A cave

4. What does the very very very big fish want to do?
a) Have the fish for his supper
b) Sit on the fish
c) Give the fish a hug

5. What does the crab think Little Fish is?
a) Kind
b) Big
c) Bad

Turn over for answers

Book Bands for Guided Reading

The Institute of Education book banding system is a scale of colours that reflects the various levels of reading difficulty. The bands are assigned by taking into account the content, the language style, the layout and phonics.

Maverick Early Readers are a bright, attractive range of books covering the pink to purple bands. All of these books have been book banded for guided reading to the industry standard and edited by a leading educational consultant.

For more titles visit:
www.maverickbooks.co.uk/early-readers

 Pink

 Red

 Yellow

 Blue

 Green

 Orange

 Turquoise

 Purple

 Book Band Yellow

Little Fish and Big Fish	978-1-84886-292-0
Sheep on the Run	978-1-84886-291-3
The Dog and the Fox	978-1-84886-293-7
Can I Have My Ball Back?	978-1-84886-252-4
Izzy! Wizzy!	978-1-84886-253-1

Quiz Answers: 1b, 2c, 3c, 4a, 5b